Longfellow Reads Longfellow

Dreams That Cannot Die

ILLUSTRATED EDITION

Poems by Henry Wadsworth Longfellow

Adapted by Layne Longfellow • Music by Michael Hoppé

For Eric,
May these lovely songs
serve you, and thru you
benefit all beings.

Acknowledgments

Coleridge said that the greatest works of art speak to the heart and the head. My mentors, Gilbert Johns and Jim McConnell, taught me that intelligent entertainment is not an oxymoron.

Providence, the Universe, and Everything, in the form (chronologically) of: Amelia's volume; Carl and Rick Piltz in volumes; Ian (who finished what he started) and Art Booth in Peggy Seeger's kitchen; Jean Anderson, in person and persistent editing; the Nine Mountain groups on the living room floor; Kathleen Shea and Ann Clark in the Wadsworth-Longfellow kitchen; Anna Sandor, midwife in Michael Hoppé's living room and consulting adult at every growth spurt since; John Etnier in his basement studio; Companion Arts Productions for *Graceful Passages*; Jim Shea, Paul Blandford, and their boom box; Paul in my ancestral graveyard in Byfield Parish, Massachusetts, and Françoise in its counterpart in Palermo, Maine; cousin Jim Lough in Phoenix at his genealogical websites; Jonathan Wyner at the console of his home away from home in Cambridge; Thomas Mikelson in his pulpit; Alisa in action; Nancy Jones, the staff and Friends of the Longfellow House; Neera for everything always; my doctors, practitioners, and Mass Mutual/Social Security Disability for keeping this dream alive.

For all those whose limitless dreams nurture their limited bodies, I speak from my heart and head to yours.

Contents

The Readings

Rhythm and Rhyme

The original texts of the poems are reprinted on the following pages with the spellings, punctuation, and line breaks reproduced exactly as they appear in Henry Wadsworth Longfellow's 1885 collected works.

Read them. Read them and relish the genteel beauty of nineteenth-century American English.

Separately, listen, and enjoy these recorded readings. The words you'll hear are not always identical to those you'll read.

I have adapted the poems for my readings, to help them roll off the tongue more fluidly, to emphasize their sound for its own sake, and for dramatic effect, searching always for the rhythms of conversation over the cadence of rhyme—for meaning and feeling over meter and form.

Improving the poems was not my purpose, and certainly I have not done so. My goal has been to make the poems easier for you to hear and to understand, as you listen instead of read.

When reading, you can linger over an unfamiliar word, a difficult passage, or a beautifully turned phrase. But when listening, lingering leads the attention astray, and the continuity of the poem is easily lost.

In listening, also, the very sound of words and phrases and constructions can be inherently pleasing. The sound of Longfellow's poems is powerful and rich; when they are read aloud, their sound enhances their meaning.

The sound of Michael Hoppé's music allows each reading to float unimpeded, its mood and its meaning mirrored by his composition.

The compositions, the adaptations, and the readings have one purpose: to recall the beauty and significance of America's most beloved classical poet, in a world of noisy competition whose purpose, often, is to divert attention from the quiet reflection these poems encourage.

We have tried to create a new work of art that derives from the work of a great man of an earlier time, to reveal the timeless.

"Washington's Head Quarters at Cambridge," (H.W. Longfellow's house), Gleason's Pictorial, *1852,*
Courtesy of the National Park Service, Longfellow National Historic Site, Cambridge, Massachusetts.

The Reading Style

"A novel by Cooper is now an antique…. Irving's world is under glass in a museum. A few fine-tuned intellectuals can still enjoy Lowell and Longfellow…."

—Guy Davenport, "Reviews," *Harper's Magazine*, June 2002.

Indeed. Here's a story that expresses the same sentiment in less finely tuned terms: It was May 2000; I sat in Coffee by Design, a few blocks from the Wadsworth-Longfellow House in Portland, Maine, with my cup and my *Collected Works*. A young man bussed the surrounding tables as I selected poems for my first recording session at the house.

"You a fan of Longfellow's?" the young voice interrupted.

"I am a Longfellow," I answered unambiguously.

"I'll never read another word of his stuff," was the matter-of-fact response. "Haven't since junior high. It's all that boring singsongy 'da-*dum* da-dum da-*dum* da-dum.'"

Perhaps a misplaced "da" here or "dum" there, but it was clear that he was intoning "By the shores of Gitche Gumee," which is where most people believe that Longfellow's great epic *Hiawatha* begins. (Actually, that line occurs well into the narrative.)

In that moment, I determined to read *Hiawatha,* and Longfellow, in such a way that listeners would not be reminded of junior high school, but would be tempted to read "another word of his stuff." So my reading style is personal, heartfelt, and conversational, disruptive of the rhythms that have come to stereotype Longfellow.

The poems seem to come from a deeper place within me than would those of another author. In any case, they are delivered from my heart, guided by the best work my mind can do—and whatever genetic benefit there might be in bearing the name of the poet.

The Art of Poetry with Music

Michael Hoppé and I began this homage to the nineteenth century in the early months of the twenty-first. This form of pairing poetry and music felt innovative at the time, and still may be, although the general idea seems to be with us in the culture now. Former Poet Laureate Robert Pinsky, for example, has performed the poetry of several eras with the Takacs String Quartet; rocker Lou Reed had a New York stage run with the poetry of Poe.

Longfellow regularly referred to his poems as "songs," and I've read them lyrically, reading especially for those who might not know America's celebrated poet. Michael Hoppé, rather than fitting melody to verse, sets each poem's meaning to music.

For those who already love and read this poetry as it was originally written—those "few fine-tuned intellectuals" of Harper's designation—we fondly hope these readings and their musical frames become beloved works in their own right.

"...the proper and immediate object of poetry is the communication of immediate pleasure."
—Coleridge, *Definitions of Poetry*, 1811.

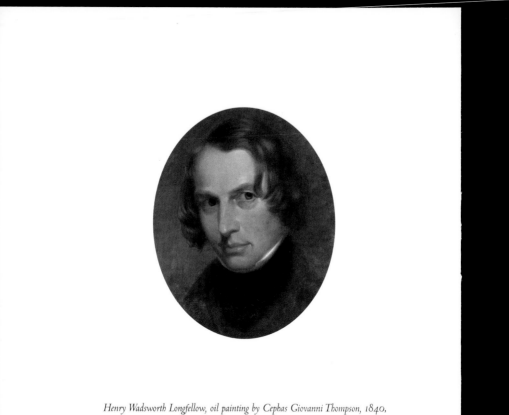

Henry Wadsworth Longfellow, oil painting by Cephas Giovanni Thompson, 1840,
Courtesy of the National Park Service, Longfellow National Historic Site, Cambridge, Massachusetts.

The Poems

The Song of Hiawatha, *perhaps more than any other poem, is responsible for Longfellow's broad popularity in his time and his continuing place in our cultural history. Dana Gioia writes that Hiawatha has become "the most popular long American poem ever written, at home and abroad." The excerpt here is from the introduction, an invocation to the world of the Native American and to this recording.*

The Song of Hiawatha.

(excerpt from the Introduction)

Ye who love a nation's legends,
Love the ballads of a people,
That like voices from afar off
Call to us to pause and listen,
Speak in tones so plain and childlike,
Scarcely can the ear distinguish
Whether they are sung or spoken;—
Listen to this Indian Legend,
To this Song of Hiawatha!

Ye whose hearts are fresh and simple,
Who have faith in God and Nature,
Who believe, that in all ages
Every human heart is human,
That in even savage bosoms
There are longings, yearnings, strivings
For the good they comprehend not,
That the feeble hands and helpless,
Groping blindly in the darkness,
Touch God's right hand in that darkness

And are lifted up and strengthened;—
Listen to this simple story,
To this Song of Hiawatha!

Ye, who sometimes, in your rambles
Through the green lanes of the country,
Where the tangled barberry-bushes
Hang their tufts of crimson berries
Over stone walls gray with mosses,
Pause by some neglected graveyard,
For a while to muse, and ponder
On a half-effaced inscription,
Written with little skill of song-craft,
Homely phrases, but each letter
Full of hope and yet of heart-break,
Full of all the tender pathos
Of the Here and the Hereafter;—
Stay and read this rude inscription,
Read this Song of Hiawatha!

Here we see creativity at work, as a personal journal entry becomes an immortal poem.

From Henry Wadsworth Longfellow's journal, September 29, 1846:

"...at the Devereux Farm by the sea-side...What a delicious scene! The ocean in the sunshine changing from the silvery hue of the thin waves upon the beach...to a thin purple on the horizon. We recalled the times past...An old-fashioned farm-house, with low rooms, and narrow windows rattling in the sea-breeze."

The Fire of Drift-Wood.
Devereux Farm, near Marblehead.

We sat within the farm-house old,
   Whose windows, looking o'er the bay,
Gave to the sea-breeze, damp and cold,
   An easy entrance, night and day.

Not far away we saw the port,
   The strange, old-fashioned, silent town,
The lighthouse, the dismantled fort,
   The wooden houses, quaint and brown.

We sat and talked until the night,
   Descending, filled the little room;
Our faces faded from the sight,
   Our voices only broke the gloom.

We spake of many a vanished scene,
   Of what we once had thought and said,
Of what had been, and might have been,
   And who was changed, and who was dead;

And all that fills the hearts of friends,
   When first they feel, with secret pain,
Their lives thenceforth have separate ends,
   And never can be one again;

The first slight swerving of the heart,
   That words are powerless to express,
And leave it still unsaid in part,
   Or say it in too great excess.

The very tones in which we spake
  Had something strange, I could but mark;
The leaves of memory seemed to make
  A mournful rustling in the dark.

Oft died the words upon our lips,
  As suddenly, from out the fire
Built of the wreck of stranded ships,
  The flames would leap and then expire,

And, as their splendor flashed and failed,
  We thought of wrecks upon the main,
Of ships dismasted, that were hailed
  And sent no answer back again.

The windows, rattling in their frames,
  The ocean, roaring up the beach,
The gusty blast, the bickering flames,
  All mingled vaguely in our speech;

Until they made themselves a part
  Of fancies floating through the brain,
The long-lost ventures of the heart,
  That send no answers back again.

O flames that glowed! O hearts that yearned!
  They were indeed too much akin,
The drift-wood fire without that burned,
  The thoughts that burned and glowed within.

Charles and Ernest Longfellow, (sons of Henry Wadsworth Longfellow), pastel by Eastman Johnson, 1848,
Courtesy of the National Park Service, Longfellow National Historic Site, Cambridge, Massachusetts.

"The Castle-Builder" was written for the poet's son, Ernest. One feels the respect for innocence that characterized Longfellow. His urging the child to hold to a direct, simple belief in the transcendent is a reaffirmation of his own belief.

The Castle-Builder.

A gentle boy, with soft and silken locks,
A dreamy boy, with brown and tender eyes,
A castle-builder, with his wooden blocks,
And towers that touch imaginary skies.

A fearless rider on his father's knee,
An eager listener unto stories told
At the Round Table of the nursery,
Of heroes and adventures manifold.

There will be other towers for thee to build;
There will be other steeds for thee to ride;
There will be other legends, and all filled
With greater marvels and more glorified.

Build on, and make thy castles high and fair,
Rising and reaching upward to the skies;
Listen to voices in the upper air,
Nor lose thy simple faith in mysteries.

"The Quadroon Girl" is one of seven antislavery poems Longfellow published in 1842, well before the issue divided the states and led to the Civil War. A telling indication of the strength of Longfellow's character comes from this letter to his father: "How do you like the slavery poems? …Some persons regret that I should have written them, but for my own part I am glad of what I have done. My feelings prompted me, and my judgment approved, and still approves." This is the very definition of integrity.

The Quadroon Girl.

The Slaver in the broad lagoon
Lay moored with idle sail;
He waited for the rising moon,
And for the evening gale.

Under the shore his boat was tied,
And all her listless crew
Watched the gray alligator slide
Into the still bayou.

Odors of orange-flowers, and spice,
Reached them from time to time,
Like airs that breathe from Paradise
Upon a world of crime.

The Planter, under his roof of thatch,

Smoked thoughtfully and slow;
The Slaver's thumb was on the latch,
He seemed in haste to go.

He said, "My ship at anchor rides
In yonder broad lagoon;
I only wait the evening tides,
And the rising of the moon."

Before them, with her face upraised,
In timid attitude,
Like one half curious, half amazed,
A Quadroon maiden stood.

Her eyes were large, and full of light,
Her arms and neck were bare;

18

No garment she wore save a kirtle bright,
   And her own long, raven hair

And on her lips there played a smile
   As holy, meek, and faint,
As lights in some cathedral aisle
   The features of a saint.

"The soil is barren,—the farm is old;"
   The thoughtful planter said;
Then looked upon the Slaver's gold,
   And then upon the maid.

His heart within him was at strife
   With such accursed gains:
For he knew whose passions gave her life,
   Whose blood ran in her veins.

But the voice of nature was too weak;
   He took the glittering gold!
Then pale as death grew the maiden's cheek,
   Her hands as icy cold.

The Slaver led her from the door,
   He led her by the hand,
To be his slave and paramour
   In a strange and distant land!

"The Children's Hour" describes a "broad hall stair" that can to this day be descended by the visitor to the Longfellow National Historic Site, just as it was by "grave Alice, and laughing Allegra, and Edith with golden hair."

The Children's Hour.

Between the dark and the daylight,
   When the night is beginning to lower,
Comes a pause in the day's occupations,
   That is known as the Children's Hour.

I hear in the chamber above me
   The patter of little feet,
The sound of a door that is opened,
   And voices soft and sweet.

From my study I see in the lamplight,
   Descending the broad hall stair,
Grave Alice, and laughing Allegra,
   And Edith with golden hair.

A whisper, and then a silence:
   Yet I know by their merry eyes
They are plotting and planning together
   To take me by surprise.

A sudden rush from the stairway,
   A sudden raid from the hall!
By three doors left unguarded
   They enter my castle wall!

They climb up into my turret
   O'er the arms and back of my chair;
If I try to escape they surround me;
   They seem to be everywhere.

They almost devour me with kisses,
   Their arms about me entwine,
Till I think of the Bishop of Bingen
   In his Mouse-Tower on the Rhine!

Do you think, O blue-eyed banditti,
   Because you have scaled the wall,
Such an old mustache as I am
   Is not a match for you all!

I have you fast in my fortress,
  And will not let you depart,
But put you down into the dungeon
  In the round-tower of my heart.

And there I will keep you forever,
  Yes, forever and a day,
Till the walls shall crumble to ruin,
  And moulder in dust away!

Three daughters of Henry Wadsworth Longfellow, oil painting by T.B. Read, 1859,
Courtesy of the National Park Service, Longfellow National Historic Site, Cambridge, Massachusetts.

Frances Appleton Longfellow, (wife of Henry Wadsworth Longfellow), drawing by Samuel Worcester Rowse, 1839, Courtesy of the National Park Service, Longfellow National Historic Site, Cambridge, Massachusetts.

"The Cross of Snow" was written on the eighteenth anniversary of the death of Longfellow's wife Fanny, and is one of two poems read here that were not published in his lifetime ("Mezzo Cammin" is the other). Both first appeared in his brother Samuel's 1886 biography of Henry. I read this poem in the room about which it is written, standing between the bed and the portrait of "a gentle face—the face of one long dead."

The Cross of Snow.

In the long, sleepless watches of the night,
 A gentle face—the face of one long dead—
 Looks at me from the wall, where round its head
 The night-lamp casts a halo of pale light.
Here in this room she died; and soul more white
 Never through martyrdom of fire was led
 To its repose; nor can in books be read
 The legend of a life more benedight.
There is a mountain in the distant West
 That, sun-defying, in its deep ravines
 Displays a cross of snow upon its side.
Such is the cross I wear upon my breast
 These eighteen years, through all the changing scenes
 And seasons, changeless since the day she died.

"The Tides" was written thirteen years after Fanny's death, and five years before "The Cross of Snow." Here, it follows "The Cross of Snow," as testament to Longfellow's resolute commitment, sometimes derided by critics, to redeem tragic events through will and perseverance.

The Tides.

I saw the long line of the vacant shore,
    The sea-weed and the shells upon the sand,
    And the brown rocks left bare on every hand,
    As if the ebbing tide would flow no more.
Then heard I, more distinctly than before,
    The ocean breathe and its great breast expand,
    And hurrying came on the defenceless land
    The insurgent waters with tumultuous roar.
All thought and feeling and desire, I said,
    Love, laughter, and the exultant joy of song
    Have ebbed from me forever! Suddenly o'er me
They swept again from their deep ocean bed,
    And in a tumult of delight, and strong
    As youth, and beautiful as youth, upbore me.

"My Lost Youth" invokes the young Henry's early life in Portland, Maine, where the Wadsworth-Longfellow House has welcomed visitors for over a century. Every poem in this collection was recorded at least once in that home, in the kitchen or in the "Rainy Day Room," where the line "Into each life some rain must fall" was written.

In his Cambridge home, the mature poet remembered: "March 29, 1855...At night, as I lie in bed, a poem comes into my mind,—a memory of Portland,—my native town, the city by the sea."

Lines from this poem ("There are things of which I may not speak; There are dreams that cannot die. . . .") were used at a critical juncture in the acclaimed 2001 film In the Bedroom.

In the early nineteenth century, Deering's Woods offered a place for a boy to roam. Today, the Friends of Deering Oaks attempt to preserve and restore the park where once the woods stood.

My Lost Youth.

Often I think of the beautiful town
   That is seated by the sea;
Often in thought go up and down
The pleasant streets of that dear old town,
   And my youth comes back to me.
      And a verse of a Lapland song
      Is haunting my memory still:
      "A boy's will is the wind's will,
And the thoughts of youth are long, long
thoughts."

I can see the shadowy lines of its trees,

   And catch, in sudden gleams,
The sheen of the far-surrounding seas,
And islands that were the Hesperides
   Of all my boyish dreams.
      And the burden of that old song,
      It murmurs and whispers still:
      "A boy's will is the wind's will,
And the thoughts of youth are long, long
thoughts."

I remember the black wharves and the slips,
   And the sea-tides tossing free;

And Spanish sailors with bearded lips,
And the beauty and mystery of the ships,
    And the magic of the sea.
        And the voice of that wayward song
        Is singing and saying still:
        "A boy's will is the wind's will,
And the thoughts of youth are long, long
thoughts."

I remember the bulwarks by the shore,
    And the fort upon the hill;
The sunrise gun, with its hollow roar,
The drum-beat repeated o'er and o'er,
    And the bugle wild and shrill.
        And the music of that old song
        Throbs in my memory still:
        "A boy's will is the wind's will,
And the thoughts of youth are long, long
thoughts."

I remember the sea-fight far away,
    How it thundered o'er the tide!
And the dead captains, as they lay
In their graves, o'erlooking the tranquil bay.

Where they in battle died.
        And the sound of that mournful song
        Goes through me with a thrill:
        "A boy's will is the wind's will,
And the thoughts of youth are long, long
thoughts."

I can see the breezy dome of groves,
    The shadows of Deering's Woods;
And the friendships old and the early loves
Come back with a Sabbath sound, as of doves
    In quiet neighborhoods.
        And the verse of that sweet old song,
        It flutters and murmurs still:
        "A boy's will is the wind's will,
And the thoughts of youth are long, long
thoughts."

I remember the gleams and glooms that dart
    Across the school-boy's brain;
The song and the silence in the heart,
That in part are prophecies, and in part
    Are longings wild and vain.
        And the voice of that fitful song

Sings on, and is never still:
    "A boy's will is the wind's will,
And the thoughts of youth are long, long thoughts."

There are things of which I may not speak;
    There are dreams that cannot die;
There are thoughts that make the strong heart weak,
And bring a pallor into the cheek,
    And a mist before the eye.
        And the words of that fatal song
        Come over me like a chill:
        "A boy's will is the wind's will,
And the thoughts of youth are long, long thoughts."

Strange to me now are the forms I meet
    When I visit the dear old town;
But the native air is pure and sweet,
And the trees that o'ershadow each well-known street,
    As they balance up and down,
        Are singing the beautiful song,

Are sighing and whispering still:
    "A boy's will is the wind's will,
And the thoughts of youth are long, long thoughts."

And Deering's Woods are fresh and fair,
    And with joy that is almost pain
My heart goes back to wander there,
And among the dreams of the days that were,
    I find my lost youth again.
        And the strange and beautiful song,
        The groves are repeating it still:
        "A boy's will is the wind's will,
And the thoughts of youth are long, long thoughts."

"Mezzo Cammin" continues our sense of Longfellow's passage through the cycle of life. This is a nineteenth-century statement of what in our time is known as "midlife crisis," when appraisal of one's life arises naturally, and a sense of failure or inadequacy is common. This poem was first published in 1886, but it was written on August 25, 1842, when Henry Longfellow was thirty-five. A century later, research found thirty-five to be the typical age for the onset of midlife wonderings.

Mezzo Cammin.

Half of my life is gone, and I have let
    The years slip from me and have not fulfilled
    The aspiration of my youth, to build
    Some tower of song with lofty parapet.
Not indolence, nor pleasure, nor the fret
    Of restless passions that would not be stilled,
    But sorrow, and a care that almost killed,
    Kept me from what I may accomplish yet;
Though, half-way up the hill, I see the Past
    Lying beneath me with its sounds and sights,—
    A city in the twilight dim and vast,
With smoking roofs, soft bells, and gleaming lights,—
    And hear above me on the autumnal blast
    The cataract of Death far thundering from the heights.

"Sonnet 1" of the Divine Comedy *is the first of two sonnets Longfellow prepared as a preface to his translation of Dante's* Inferno. *Longfellow's younger brother and biographer, Samuel, was a Unitarian minister; Henry's daughter Alice described her father as a lifelong Unitarian. Thomas Mikelson, the current Pastor of the First Parish Unitarian Universalist Church in Cambridge, Massachusetts, the church Henry attended, says, "The reference to himself as 'unashamed to pray' points to his understanding of the clear choice intellectuals like himself felt in choosing traditional reverence, and it also announces his choice—he was unashamed to pray."*

Sonnet I.
Divine Comedy

Oft have I seen at some cathedral door
   A laborer, pausing in the dust and heat,
   Lay down his burden, and with reverent feet
   Enter, and cross himself, and on the floor
Kneel to repeat his paternoster o'er;
   Far off the noises of the world retreat;
   The loud vociferations of the street
   Become an undistinguishable roar.
So, as I enter here from day to day,
   And leave my burden at this minster gate,
   Kneeling in prayer, and not ashamed to pray,
The tumult of the time disconsolate
   To inarticulate murmurs dies away,
   While the eternal ages watch and wait.

"The Slave's Dream" is the second of the two antislavery poems in this collection. Longfellow's commitment to their principles is made clear in my earlier notes to "The Quadroon Girl." His closest friend, Charles Sumner, was a prominent abolitionist, and their correspondence shows Longfellow's support of his friend's activism. The range of Longfellow's understanding of the issue is manifest in these two poems—one about the hapless plantation girl of mixed blood, the other about the proud and accomplished Nigerian King, their disparate stations not preventing their shared fate.

The Slave's Dream.

Beside the ungathered rice he lay,
   His sickle in his hand;
His breast was bare, his matted hair
   Was buried in the sand.
Again, in the mist and shadow of sleep,
   He saw his Native Land.

Wide through the landscape of his dreams
   The lordly Niger flowed;
Beneath the palm-trees on the plain
   Once more a king he strode;
And heard the tinkling caravans
   Descend the mountain-road.

He saw once more his dark-eyed queen
   Among her children stand;

They clasped his neck, they kissed his cheeks,
   They held him by the hand!—
A tear burst from the sleeper's lids
   And fell into the sand.

And then at furious speed he rode
   Along the Niger's bank;
His bridle-reins were golden chains,
   And, with a martial clank,
At each leap he could feel his scabbard of steel
   Smiting his stallion's flank.

Before him, like a blood-red flag,
   The bright flamingoes flew;
From morn till night he followed their flight,
   O'er plains where the tamarind grew,

Till he saw the roofs of Caffre huts,
   And the ocean rose to view.

At night he heard the lion roar,
   And the hyena scream,
And the river-horse, as he crushed the reeds
   Beside some hidden stream;
And it passed, like a glorious roll of drums,
   Through the triumph of his dream.

The forests, with their myriad tongues,
   Shouted of liberty;
And the Blast of the Desert cried aloud,
   With a voice so wild and free,
That he started in his sleep and smiled
   At their tempestuous glee.

He did not feel the driver's whip,
   Nor the burning heat of day;
For Death had illumined the Land of Sleep,
   And his lifeless body lay
A worn-out fetter, that the soul
   Had broken and thrown away!

"Sonnet 4" is the second of two sonnets Longfellow prepared for the preface to Dante's Purgatorio. *This work and "The Cross of Snow" were the most difficult for me to read to my own satisfaction, perhaps because they are so personal, so romantically revealing. Two years separated my first readings of them, in the kitchen of the Portland Wadsworth-Longfellow House, and my last series, begun in the master bedroom of Longfellow's Cambridge home.*

Sonnet 4.
Divine Comedy

With snow-white veil and garments as of flame,
    She stands before thee, who so long ago
    Filled thy young heart with passion and the woe
    From which thy song and all its splendors came;
And while with stern rebuke she speaks thy name,
    The ice about thy heart melts as the snow
    On mountain heights, and in swift overflow
    Comes gushing from thy lips in sobs of shame.
Thou makest full confession; and a gleam,
    As if the dawn on some dark forest cast,
    Seems on thy lifted forehead to increase;
Lethe and Eunoë—the remembered dream
    And the forgotten sorrow—bring at last
    That perfect pardon which is perfect peace.

"Three Friends of Mine" offers a delightful notion of the afterlife—dear friends who have preceded you in death might remember you in Paradise, and smile when they do. The three friends of whom Longfellow writes were Cornelius Conway Felton, Louis Agassiz, and Charles Sumner, who passed in 1862, 1873, and 1874, respectively. 1874 was the year of the poem's publication, eight years before the end of Longfellow's life.

Three Friends of Mine.

When I remember them, those friends of mine,
    Who are no longer here, the noble three,
    Who half my life were more than friends to me,
    And whose discourse was like a generous wine,
I most of all remember the divine
    Something, that shone in them, and made us see
    The archetypal man, and what might be
    The amplitude of Nature's first design.
In vain I stretch my hands to clasp their hands;
    I cannot find them. Nothing now is left
    But a majestic memory. They meanwhile
Wander together in Elysian lands,
    Perchance remembering me, who am bereft
    Of their dear presence, and, remembering, smile.

Tales of a Wayside Inn *was written and published in segments over the years 1863-73 and subsequently gathered into one set of tales, of which the best known is "The Landlord's Tale—Paul Revere's Ride." I have chosen from the Prelude, to set the stage for the listener to be invited to Sudbury and to the Wayside Inn, which still receives the traveler warmly.*

Tales of a Wayside Inn.
Prelude
The Wayside Inn

One Autumn night, in Sudbury town,
Across the meadows bare and brown,
The windows of the wayside inn
Gleamed red with fire-light through the
leaves
Of woodbine, hanging from the eaves
Their crimson curtains rent and thin

As ancient is this hostelry
As any in the land may be,
Built in the old Colonial day,
When men lived in a grander way,
With ampler hospitality;
A kind of old Hobgoblin Hall,
Now somewhat fallen to decay,

With weather stains upon the wall,
And stairways worn, and crazy doors,
And creaking and uneven floors,
And chimneys huge, and tiled and tall.

A region of repose it seems,
A place of slumber and of dreams,
Remote among the wooded hills!
For there no noisy railway speeds,
Its torch-race scattering smoke and gleeds;
But noon and night, the panting teams
Stop under the great oaks, that throw
Tangles of light and shade below,
On roofs and doors and window-sills.
Across the road the barns display

Their lines of stalls, their mows of hay,
Through the wide doors the breezes blow,
The wattled cocks strut to and fro,
And, half effaced by rain and shine,
The Red Horse prances on the sign.

Round this old-fashioned, quaint abode
Deep silence reigned, save when a gust
Went rushing down the country road,
And skeletons of leaves, and dust,
A moment quickened by its breath,
Shuddered and danced their dance of death,
And through the ancient oaks o'erhead
Mysterious voices moaned and fled.

But from the parlor of the inn
A pleasant murmur smote the ear,
Like water rushing through a weir:
Oft interrupted by the din
Of laughter and of loud applause,
And, in each intervening pause,
The music of a violin.
The fire-light, shedding over all
The splendor of its ruddy glow,

Filled the whole parlor large and low;
It gleamed on wainscot and on wall,
It touched with more than wonted grace
Fair Princess Mary's pictured face;
It bronzed the rafters overhead,
On the old spinet's ivory keys
It played inaudible melodies,
It crowned the somber clock with flame,
The hands, the hours, the maker's name
And painted with a livelier red
The Landlord's coat-of-arms again;
And, flashing on the window-pane,
Emblazoned with its light and shade
The jovial rhymes, that still remain,
Writ near a century ago,
By the great Major Molineaux,
Whom Hawthorne has immortal made.

Before the blazing fire of wood
Erect the rapt musician stood;
And ever and anon he bent
His head upon his instrument,
And seemed to listen till he caught
Confessions of its secret thought,—

The joy, the triumph, the lament,
The exultation and the pain;
Then, by the magic of his art,
He soothed the throbbings of its heart,
And lulled it into peace again.

"The Broken Oar," though published in 1876, has reference in Longfellow's diary of November 13, 1864: "I am frequently tempted to write upon my work the inscription found upon an oar cast on the coast of Iceland,—'Oft was I weary when I tugged at thee.'" On January 9, 1863, his journal reads, "I am ashamed to lead so useless and listless a life." A prolific writer under all moods and circumstances, Longfellow clearly felt the burden of his work. Thus he closes this poem with the tossing of the poet's useless pen into the sea, representing his abiding questioning of the contribution of the poet and the poems.

The Broken Oar.

Once upon Iceland's solitary strand
    A poet wandered with his book and pen,
    Seeking some final word, some sweet Amen,
    Wherewith to close the volume in his hand.
The billows rolled and plunged upon the sand,
    The circling sea-gulls swept beyond his ken,
    And from the parting cloud-rack now and then
    Flashed the red sunset over sea and land.
Then by the billows at his feet was tossed
    A broken oar; and carved thereon he read,
    "Oft was I weary, when I toiled at thee;"
And like a man, who findeth what was lost,
    He wrote the words, then lifted up his head,
    And flung his useless pen into the sea.

"The Tide Rises, The Tide Falls" is a statement of our transitory existence, the impermanence of our imprint, and the imperturbable continuity of Nature, as "the eternal ages watch and wait."

The Tide Rises, The Tide Falls.

The tide rises, the tide falls,
The twilight darkens, the curlew calls;
Along the sea-sands damp and brown
The traveller hastens toward the town,
   And the tide rises, the tide falls.

Darkness settles on roofs and walls,
But the sea in the darkness calls and calls;
The little waves, with their soft, white hands,
Efface the footprints in the sands,
   And the tide rises, the tide falls.

The morning breaks; the steeds in their stalls
Stamp and neigh, as the hostler calls;
The day returns, but nevermore
Returns the traveller to the shore,
   And the tide rises, the tide falls.

"The Meeting" is an anthem for class reunions, for the parting of old friends, for gatherings of family and friends at holidays—and for the sense of longing that inevitably accompanies the dropping away, through death or departure, of those who knit the fabric of one's life.

The Meeting.

After so long an absence
   At last we meet again:
Does the meeting give us pleasure,
   Or does it give us pain?

The tree of life has been shaken,
   And but few of us linger now,
Like the Prophet's two or three berries
   In the top of the uppermost bough.

We cordially greet each other
   In the old, familiar tone;
And we think, though we do not say it,
   How old and gray he has grown!

We speak of a Merry Christmas
   And many a Happy New Year;
But each in his heart is thinking
   Of those that are not here.

We speak of friends and their fortunes,
   And of what they did and said,
Till the dead alone seem living,
   And the living alone seem dead.

And at last we hardly distinguish
   Between the ghosts and the guests;
And a mist and shadow of sadness
   Steals over our merriest jests.

Evangeline is at once a great epic poem, a loosely historical document, the making of a myth, and a measure of Longfellow's social consciousness. Hiawatha *memorializes the eviction of the Native American by the European;* Evangeline *tells of the eviction by the English of French villagers from their homes in "Acadia," now northern Maine and Nova Scotia. Many migrated to French Louisiana, where "Acadians" evolved into our word "Cajuns." Longfellow immortalized these historical events through the tale of two young lovers, forcibly separated as they prepare to marry, who spend their remaining lives searching for each other.*

I have chosen from the closing segment of the poem, as a fitting close to the album. Some critics have expressed disappointment in Longfellow's having completed such a grand work with an openly sentimental ending, as close to a "happy ending" as possible under the circumstances. For me, it is an elegant statement of idealized devotion. I required several readings to get through a recording without audibly choking up. I am a hopeful romantic; it runs in the family.

Evangeline.

[Evangeline entered the door of the poorhouse]
Suddenly, as if arrested by fear or a feeling of wonder,
Still she stood, with her colorless lips apart, while a shudder
Ran through her frame, and, forgotten, the flowerets dropped from her fingers,
And from her eyes and cheeks the light and bloom of the morning.
Then there escaped from her lips a cry of such terrible anguish,
That the dying heard it, and started up from their pillows.
On the pallet before her was stretched the form of an old man.
Long, and thin, and gray were the locks that shaded his temples;
But, as he lay in the morning light, his face for a moment

Seemed to assume once more the forms of its earlier manhood;
So are wont to be changed the faces of those who are dying.
Hot and red on his lips still burned the flush of the fever,
As if life, like the Hebrew, with blood had besprinkled its portals,
That the Angel of Death might see the sign, and pass over.
Motionless, senseless, dying, he lay, and his spirit exhausted
Seemed to be sinking down through infinite depths in the darkness,
Darkness of slumber and death, forever sinking and sinking,
Then through those realms of shade, in multiplied reverberations,
Heard he that cry of pain, and through the hush that succeeded
Whispered a gentle voice, in accents tender and saint-like,
"Gabriel! O my beloved!" and died away into silence.
Then he beheld, in a dream, once more the home of his childhood;
Green Acadian meadows, with sylvan rivers among them,
Village, and mountain, and woodlands; and, walking under their shadow,
As in the days of her youth, Evangeline rose in his vision.
Tears came into his eyes; and as slowly he lifted his eyelids,
Vanished the vision away, but Evangeline knelt by his bedside.
Vainly he strove to whisper her name, for the accents unuttered
Died on his lips, and their motion revealed what his tongue would have spoken.
Vainly he strove to rise; and Evangeline, kneeling beside him,
Kissed his dying lips, and laid his head on her bosom.
Sweet was the light of his eyes; but it suddenly sank into darkness,
As when a lamp is blown out by a gust of wind at a casement.

All was ended now, the hope, and the fear, and the sorrow,
All the aching of heart, the restless, unsatisfied longing,
All the dull deep pain, and constant anguish of patience!
And, as she pressed once more the lifeless head to her bosom,
Meekly she bowed her own, and murmured, "Father, I thank thee!"

The Poet

The Poet Today

The name "Longfellow" is my personal measure of the poet's declining stature in the culture whose prevailing myths he helped create. In the *New York Times* and *Los Angeles Times* book review sections, in scholarly volumes on the history of poetry, even on CNN.com, writers from Dana Gioia to Stanley Kunitz have weighed in on Longfellow's greatness or lack thereof, and his place in our cultural pantheon.

Here's what it has felt like up close and personal:

When I was growing up, the inevitable response to my last name was, "Are you related to the poet?"

By the time I started college, the Modernists' disdain for Longfellow's Victorian gentility, accessible storytelling, and lack of self-obsessiveness had taken over. On the first day of my Freshman year, my Honors English professor peered over his half-glasses and queried,

"Are you related...?"

"Yes," I hopefully replied.

"Pity he wasn't a better poet," he said, and dismissed both Longfellows to the intransigence of time and mode.

Time has not been kind. The characteristic response to "My name is Longfellow" shifted, in recent generations, from any reference to the poet to "How do you spell that?"

Or, from a college student in Boston, taking my public radio pledge: "Longfellow—is that all one word?"

And, while recording at the Longfellow National Historic Site, I had a pleasant interaction with a shopkeeper. Upon learning my name, he surmised that I must be related to the Longfellow Bridge that connects Cambridge to Boston. The bridge itself, that is, not to the poet for whom the bridge was long ago named. Even for a man so honored and so loved, "the tide rises and the tide falls."

Henry Wadsworth Longfellow, pastel portrait by Samuel Lawrence, 1854,
Courtesy of the Longfellow National Historic Site, Cambridge, Massachusetts.

The Poet

Henry Wadsworth Longfellow was born in Portland, Maine, in 1807. He became the best-selling, most widely quoted American author in an era in which poets were accorded the status now reserved for rock stars. Remarkably, while topping the bestseller lists of the nineteenth century, Longfellow held international stature as a scholar. He spoke seven languages and understood nearly twice that number. His translation of Dante's *Divine Comedy* was utilized (and complimented, both for its art and its accuracy) 125 years after its original publication, by American Poet Laureate Robert Pinsky, in his own translation of Dante.

Longfellow was appointed Professor of Modern Languages at Bowdoin College at age eighteen, immediately upon graduation from that institution. By age twenty-seven, he accepted the Smith Chair in Modern Languages at Harvard University.

He vacated that position in 1854, in part to escape the demands on his time and energies, but also because, to put it directly, he did not need the salary to supplement his income from his poetry—he was paid as much as $3000 for a poem.

Personally, he was a great and good friend, a fine family man, and a loyal and gracious correspondent. He responded to a great many of the unsolicited letters he received from an admiring but unknown public, although his journals reveal the degree of imposition that placed on him.

He married Mary Storer Potter in 1831. She accompanied him on his second European trip, which he undertook in order to prepare himself for his Harvard position. His young wife died in Rotterdam of complications following a miscarriage.

In 1843 he married Frances Appleton, whose father purchased the Craigie House near Harvard for them as a wedding present. Longfellow had boarded in the house, which already had an illustrious history—it had served as Washington's Revolutionary War headquarters for a time. Today, it is the Longfellow National Historic Site, recently restored to former glory, administered by the National Park Service, and welcoming visitors.

Frances Appleton Longfellow—Fanny—died tragically in 1861. She was sealing a package of locks of hair from her daughters when her light summer dress caught fire from a match. She ran to her husband, who attempted to smother the flames with a rug. She died the next day. Longfellow was unable to attend her burial due to the severity of his own burns. These burns were the occasion for growing the full beard that we commonly associate with him.

The Wadsworth-Longfellow House, Portland, Maine.

Henry Wadsworth Longfellow, detail of an oil painting by George P.A. Healy, 1862,
Courtesy of the National Park Service, Longfellow National Historic Site, Cambridge, Massachusetts.

The Reader

The Reader

Layne Longfellow created Lecture Theatre^{sm}, presenting keynote lectures throughout North America and abroad. Elected to the International Speakers Hall of Fame in 1986, he was an innovator in using live and recorded music, humor, poetry, photographs, and video as context for academic theory and data.

His 1983 "Beyond Success" presentation was recently selected among the twelve best of the past twenty-five years. "The Mountain Waits," a CBC documentary of his Banff Centre (Canada) mountaineering seminar for executives, was awarded the Gold Medal for Outdoor Films at the New York Festival of TV and Film. He is the author of *Imaginary Menagerie*, a children's book, *Visual Feast*, a book of visual puns (both Chronicle Books), several Lecture Theatre audios and videos, and cocreator of "Body Talk" and "Feel Wheel," psychological games that were released by *Psychology Today* for professional use. His most recent written work, "The Language of Commerce Interprets Living Systems," is in *Discourses in Search of Members* (University Press of America, 2002). His early neuro-psychological research appeared in *Science*.

He received a B.A. (Ohio University) and Ph.D. (University of Michigan) in experimental psychology, with fellowships from the National Science and Woodrow Wilson Foundations; an NIMH Post-Doctoral Fellowship supported his two years of work with Dr. Carl Rogers.

He served as Director of Executive Seminars at The Menninger Foundation, Academic Vice President of Prescott College, and on the faculty of Reed College.

Layne Longfellow graduated from Jackson High School in Jackson, Ohio, in the foothills of Appalachia. His great-great-grandfather Michael Longfellow migrated to southern Ohio from Maine, coincident with Henry Longfellow's leaving Maine for Harvard.

www.laynelongfellow.com

The Family Connection

William Longfellow, the first Longfellow in North America, was born in 1650 in Horsforth, Yorkshire, England, near Leeds. In 1676 he emigrated to northeastern Massachusetts, and in 1678 married Anne Sewall. They had six children.

Their fourth child was Stephen; their sixth child was Nathan. Stephen's great-great-grandson was Henry Wadsworth Longfellow. Nathan's great-great-great-great-great-great-grandson is Layne Longfellow.

Of Henry's five children who survived to adulthood, Anne Allegra and Edith continued the family line.

Henry Wadsworth Longfellow, detail of a photograph by Notman and Campbell, 1880,
Courtesy of the National Park Service, Longfellow National Historic Site, Cambridge, Massachusetts.

The Music

The Composer

Michael Hoppé is an English composer, born in Egypt, who currently lives in Los Angeles. His music has been heard on programs ranging from HBO's *The Sopranos* to *The Oprah Winfrey Show;* he has scored feature films including *Misunderstood* and *Eyes of the Wind.* His recordings were the official music for the Palm Springs and Santa Barbara International Film Festivals, and his music has been extensively used in workshops by authors such as Julia Cameron, Sarah Breathnach, and Robert Cooper. Hoppé's songs have been recorded by a variety of performers, including Tim Wheater, Martin Tillman, Zamfir, Frank Mills, Eliza Gilkyson, Louise Di Tullio, and Eugene Fodor. His work in the music industry has brought him several gold and platinum records. As a senior executive at Polygram, he was responsible for signing such diverse talents as Vangelis, The Who, Kitaro, Jean-Michel Jarre, and ABBA. His albums "The Yearning" and "Afterglow" won AFIM Awards as "CD of the Year" and "Best New Age Album," respectively. His previous albums can be found in stores internationally and at:

www.michaelhoppe.com

hoppe@thegrid.net.

The Musicians

All music produced, arranged, and composed by Michael Hoppé, except "The Song of Hiawatha," by Michael Hoppé and Tim Wheater.

Michael Hoppé — Keyboards
Martin Tillman — Cello
Xin Hua — Cello
Tim Wheater — Flutes
Heidi Fielding — Soprano
Kenton Youngstrom — Guitar
Chris Bleth — Oboe
James Sitterly — Violin
Harold Moses — Viola

Music published by Chordially Yours Music (ASCAP).

The Recordings

All poems were recorded in the Wadsworth-Longfellow House, Portland, Maine, and the Longfellow National Historic Site, Cambridge, Massachusetts.

We offer our gratitude for their gracious hospitality and the irreplaceable opportunity they afforded us.

Additional recording sessions were done principally by John Etnier, at Studio Dual, Portland, Maine. Supplemental recording was done at Coupe Studios, Boulder, Colorado.

Michael Hoppé donned his headphones, surrounded himself with the recorded reading, and in turn surrounded the reading with music.

Mixing and mastering were then done by Jonathan Wyner and Layne Longfellow at MWorks Studios, Cambridge, Massachusetts.

I am indebted to Jonathan, John, and Michael for their their expertise, their reliability, and their aesthetic.

The Sources

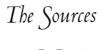

Sources from the reader's personal collection:

Longfellow, Henry Wadsworth. *The Complete Poetical Works of Henry W. Longfellow.* London: Great Book Establishment, 1856.

————. *The Poetical Works of Henry Wadsworth Longfellow.* Cambridge: The Riverside Press, 1885.

————. *Henry Wadsworth Longfellow: Complete Poems.* Cutchogue, NY: Buccaneer Press, 1993.

Longfellow, Samuel. *Life of Henry Wadsworth Longfellow and Final Memorials of Henry Wadsworth Longfellow.* Boston: Ticknor and Company, 1886-1887.

The texts of the poems are from the 1885 volume above.

The marbled papers are reproduced from the 1886-87 volumes above.

The engraved illustrations are from the 1856, 1885, and 1886 volumes above.

Additional sources:

CNN. "Longfellow's home, reputation rehabilitated." September 18, 2000. [Available on-line: http://www.cnn.com/2000/STYLE/design/09/18/longfellow.house.ap]

Gioia, Dana. "Longfellow in the aftermath of Modernism" (in *The Columbia History of American Poetry,* Jay Parini, ed.). New York: MJF Books, 1993.

McClatchy, J.D. "Return to Gitche Gumee," *New York Times Book Review.* October 22, 2000, p. 39.

Trachtenberg, Alan. "Longfellow's Radical Americanism," *Los Angeles Times Book Review,* December 10, 2000, pp. 4-5.

Liner notes, commentaries, album and book concepts by Layne Longfellow.

Graphic design by Glenna Lang.